AGING WITH GRACE

ACCEPTANCE & GRATITUDE

BURT NORDSTRAND

with Carol Pine

ISBN 979-8-218-87562-6
Library of Congress Catalog Number: 2025925175
First edition 2026
Printed in the United States of America

Cover photo: Burt Nordstrand

Design: Blue Hot Creative

Portions of the 12 Steps of Alcoholics Anonymous are from *Alcoholics Anonymous*, Fourth Edition, Alcoholics Anonymous World Services, Inc., 2001.

Portions of the 12 Steps of Overeaters Anonymous are from *Overeaters Anonymous*, Overeaters Anonymous, Inc., 1980.

For Yvonne

The love of my life for over 35 years
And still my greatest gift—
My companion through every season.

CONTENTS

INTRODUCTION
A WORD FROM THE AUTHOR

This book is a continuation of my autobiography, *Living with the Enemy*. Writing that first book—and now continuing with *Aging with Grace*—has been a deeply rewarding process. In many ways, it feels much like step four of my lifelong program, which calls us to make "a searching and fearless moral inventory of ourselves." That practice of reflection and honesty has shaped both my life and my writing.

I often hear it said that aging is not for the faint of heart. I have found this to be true. Yet, if one accepts it, aging can also be an unexpectedly rich and even interesting journey. It demands courage, patience, and—above all—a willingness to let go.

For me, the practice of letting go became very real after the challenges of COVID and then long COVID in 2020 and 2021. During that time, I had to release many of the athletic activities that had once defined me—mountain road biking, hiking, and so much more. These were not small losses; they were threads of my identity. But with each letting go came a new opportunity: to discover different ways of living, of being, and of finding grace in the life I still have.

A year or two later, glaucoma forced me to surrender yet another part of myself: the lifelong passion and lifestyle of sailing. After more than forty years of owning and sailing yachts in the Caribbean, I had to let that chapter close. Soon after, I also had to give up driving—a freedom I had taken for granted since youth. These were not easy adjustments. Each loss felt like another reminder that time was changing me in ways I could not control.

And yet, through all of this, I have learned that aging is not simply about what we leave behind, but about what we gain in wisdom, resilience, and perspective. It is about practicing acceptance daily, finding gratitude in what remains, and learning to embrace a slower, gentler rhythm of life.

This book, *Aging with Grace*, is both a reflection and an offering. It is my attempt to face aging honestly, to share what it has taken from me and what it has given in return, and to remind myself—and perhaps you, the reader—that even in loss, there can be grace.

ABOUT THE AUTHORS

More than 47 years ago at age 40, **Burt Nordstrand** began his recovery from compulsive overeating and alcoholism. He was a successful entrepreneur who transformed the self-service gasoline and convenience store industry and, in 2016, sold his company, SSG Corporation, for more than $50 million. Over the years, he also developed, owned and operated multiple commercial real estate development properties. In 2011, Nordstrand created COR Retreat, an affordable, residential, 12-Step recovery program for food addicts and, by 2025, COR had served more than 2,300 people from around the United States and the world. At age 87, Nordstrand reflects on the challenges—and gifts—of aging in this honest and practical account that anyone will find inspiring.

Carol Pine has been a professional writer and business journalist for 50 years. She has written 48 corporate history and business biographies and authored prize-winning business columns for the Saint Paul *Pioneer Press* newspaper and *Corporate Report* magazine. She started her career as a weekly newspaper editor in suburban Minneapolis. For 15 years, she served as an adjunct professor at the University of Minnesota Hubbard School of Journalism, her alma mater. Carol is in long-term recovery from alcoholism and lives full time in Savannah, Georgia where she co-founded a non-profit: the Interfaith Addiction and Recovery Coalition.

ACKNOWLEDGMENTS

My deepest gratitude goes to my family and close friends who have made this life possible—who have made *Aging with Grace* not only possible, but meaningful and deeply rewarding.

First and foremost, to the love of my life and my partner, Yvonne. We met a couple years after I found recovery through the Twelve Step program, and from that moment she has been my steadfast companion through every joy and challenge. Together, we have learned what it means to share a life built on trust, laughter, humility, and love. I remain profoundly grateful for the grace we continue to discover together.

To our five extraordinary children—Jennie, John, Anne Marie, Katie, and Brian—thank you for filling our lives with light, patience, and purpose. We like to say that none of our children are genetically related, yet each of you is wholly and beautifully our own. Some are adopted, some are biological, but in every way that matters, we are one family, bound not by blood, but by love.

To our children's partners—Jane, Tammy, Aaron, Rob, and Jordan—thank you for loving and supporting our children, and for expanding our family with your warmth, humor, and kindness. You have each added your own light to our lives, and we are deeply grateful to share this journey with you.

To our grandchildren—Nick, Sam, Ikey, Michael, Gabe, Seth, Sonny, Samara, Murphy, Jack, Les, and Joel—you are the living proof of love carried forward. Each of you brings joy, curiosity, and energy into our world, reminding us that grace is renewed in every generation. Watching you grow has been one of the great blessings of our lives.

And to my oldest grandsons Nick and Sam, now building lives of their own with their partners, Becky and Chloe, we celebrate the continuation of love through you—the next chapter of our family's story unfolding with hope and grace.

A special thank-you to my dear friends who have shared this life's journey with me—from those quiet, early-morning cockpit conversations aboard my sailboat, *Serenity*, to the many hours of laughter, reflection, and truth we've shared along the way. You have each helped me see life more clearly and live it more gratefully.

To my Twelve Step sponsors—Tim, Steve, and Bob—thank you for walking this path of aging with grace beside me. Your friendship, wisdom, and example have been steady guides on this ongoing journey of recovery and renewal.

And finally, to all who have walked beside us, encouraged us, and believed in the beauty of growing older with compassion and courage—thank you. This book exists because of you.

AGING WITH GRACE: REFLECTIONS ON LIFE, LOVE AND LETTING GO

I did not plan on getting old, but I turned 87 in December, 2025. For most of my professional life, I was the youngest person in the room and yet I was the company president, the owner, the tenacious entrepreneur. I gambled and made things happen, building my business from virtually nothing, pushing myself hard and moving at warp speed. I was an accomplished con artist—a skill I developed early.

I was also an addict. I did virtually everything to excess in my first 40 years of life, so my longevity was not guaranteed.

Fortunately, I found recovery from my two primary addictions: compulsive overeating and alcoholism.

I have spent decades thinking of others as old, and now—thanks to recovery—I have become an elder. I understand the science of aging and how it works within my own body: I am not so sharp, spry or athletic as I once was and I am reminded daily of how age is changing me.

I returned from a sailing trip in the Caribbean with my family and I discovered that I cannot jump in and out of the dinghy or spot the steps on the marina dock as I once did.

I need a helper to assist me because I'm losing my eyesight. At times, I struggle to hear conversations.

I have to practice acceptance every day!

"Help him with his suitcase," I heard a mom tell her son as I prepared to exit an airplane. Was she really talking about me?

FEWER SUNSETS

Brazilian poet and novelist Mário de Andrade wrote this about aging before his death in 1945:

"*I counted my years*
And realized that I have
Less time to live by
Than I have lived so far.
I feel like a child who won a pack of candies:
At first he ate them with pleasure, but when he realized that there was little left, he began to taste them intensely.
We have two lives…
And the second begins
When you realize
You only have one."

The reality of aging can be stunning, scary and even a little sad for all of us, especially when we recognize that we have far less time ahead. There are fewer sunsets and less time to watch my grandchildren grow up. Combine this reality with increasing losses of people I love: my dearest friends, my parents, my younger brother Ron, who passed away in 2019 and recently, my older brother Dennis, who almost reached 90.

Now, I'm the family patriarch. I am reminded of my own diminishing "shelf life" with each doctor visit, exam and diagnosis.

I am losing my battle with glaucoma: I am blind in my right eye and down to 20 percent vision in my left eye.

You might expect me to be a grumpy old man, but I am not. I'm still here and grateful for my eight decades.

The way I lived my first 40 years—which I will describe—could easily have resulted in an early death or—at the very least—a debilitating disease, unless I changed dramatically.

I did change.

'GROWING UP IS OPTIONAL'

In early life, I was powerless over my addictive behaviors and ways of thinking. I faced those foes with a lot of help from caring people. I was introduced to a 12-Step program, a practice that anyone can adopt. Recovery gave me a straightforward, realistic and positive way to address every issue in life. All I had to do was "work the Steps," and recognize a "Higher Power" in my life that I alone chose. I call that power God.

I must remember—at all times—that this Higher Power is *not* me. Not ever. Today, my spiritual connection is almost as automatic as breathing. God is clearly in the front seat of my two-seater bicycle and I (mostly) let Him steer.

Recovery from addiction has changed me. It has saved my life and extended my life so that I can accept aging with gratitude and hope, where there once was control and fear. I continue to discover more about life and myself.

Even at 87, I am still becoming the person I was always meant to be—free from the curse of addiction. I like what Walt Disney said about aging: "Growing old is mandatory, but growing *up* is optional."

I have been given the courage to face my own aging, the real possibility of going blind and my ultimate death. Similarly, I have been given the gift of time to appreciate longevity.

STEPPING UP

The simply-stated "recovery steps" (page 109) that guide my daily life have been around for 90 years since 1935. They are practiced all over the world and they can alter any life for the better, whether you suffer from addiction or not.

These 12 Steps were first developed by a surgeon and a stock broker in Akron, Ohio, who were both hopeless alcoholics. The two men sought a way to find recovery for themselves and others. They knew their lives would end too soon without embracing change. But how? Their solution was the creation of Alcoholics Anonymous (A.A.), a free program that welcomes everyone and relies on sharing personal stories and mutual support in a confidential setting.

A.A. members have this in common: they are powerless over alcohol and their lives have become unmanageable. The 12 Steps have been applied to more than 30 self-help recovery programs including, but not limited to, adult children of alcoholics, gamblers, food addicts, drug addicts, smokers, sex addicts and workaholics.

I believe that every person is powerless over something (or someone) and that includes our own aging.

STAYING AWAKE

I have enjoyed nearly 50 additional years that the 40-year-old Burt Nordstrand—had he continued his reckless life course—never would have experienced.

Some of our peers laugh and say, "If I'd known I was going to live this long, I would have taken better care of myself!" Whether it was sheer luck, divine guidance, or both, I'm still here. Now I want to share how my life has changed, lengthened and how I'm accepting aging.

Perhaps my story will be of value to you.

I am a grateful man in my eighth decade who is opening his life for anyone to see by telling the truth about my own vulnerability, impermanence and, yes, even my irrelevance. I aim to be an honest witness about aging. Whether I last two more years or twenty-two, I commit to being "aware and awake" as author, philosopher and spiritual teacher Eckhart Tolle says—especially as I face my loss of independence, an increasingly fragile body and my inevitable death.

Tolle says that the most effective way to become aware and awake is through a mutual aid program—in your church, synagogue or mosque, in a men's or women's group, through therapy or pursuing another form of honest self-discovery.

For me, it is my 12-Step program that helps me examine daily what I might resist. I believe that what makes aging unbearable are my attempts to deny aging. I am dedicated to living in the present and staying awake instead of being fearful, so that I can open my heart deeply to this final experience of life and embrace the people I love.

FEAR OR FAITH?

Here is what I have learned about fear. It comes from *Daily Reflections*, a book used by many in 12-Step programs. Bill W., the co-founder of Alcoholics Anonymous, wrote this:

"The achievement of freedom from fear is a lifetime undertaking, one that can never be wholly completed. When under heavy attack, in acute illness, or facing other conditions of serious insecurity, we shall all react to this emotion—well or badly, as the case may be. Only the self-deceived will claim perfect freedom from fear.

"Fear has caused me suffering when I could have had more faith. There are times when fear suddenly tears me apart, just when I'm experiencing feelings of joy, happiness and a lightness of heart.

"Faith—and a feeling of self-worth toward a Higher Power—helps me endure tragedy and ecstasy. When I choose to give all of my fears over to my Higher Power, I will be free."

This honest statement by the co-founder of A.A. is true for me at all times.

I care about every day now, knowing that God is doing for me what I cannot do for myself. I am in good hands. I know that happiness is not imagining a better future. Happiness exists in the *here and now*. This mindset helps me to live freely, to love more deeply and to forgive more quickly—while accepting life's additions and subtractions with grace.

THE VERTICAL PATH

Eckhart Tolle writes about living life on two paths: a vertical path and a horizontal path. The vertical is a straight path upward: we are born happy, we live 60 to 90-plus years, we die happy and our soul returns to the God of our understanding. This path is about conscious awareness and the constant presence of a Higher Power. I have learned that the best way to remain on this vertical path is to honor my true self-worth, live in the present moment, be aware and realize the presence of the God of my understanding through meditation and silence. This practice did not come easily to the hard-driving entrepreneur fueled by addiction, but I am living proof that dramatic change is possible.

"True-self worth comes directly from the realization of the Being that you are, which is precious," Tolle says. "There is a sense of infinite worth or worthiness that does not depend on any comparison. You are the sacredness of life itself. Ultimately, the only real success in life is how conscious you are and how much consciousness is manifesting, emerging and shining through you in the here and now.

"Most humans are unaware of the vertical path," Tolle says. "All they have is the horizontal path and time dominates that dimension. Time is often perceived as a wonderful thing: there are things to do, to achieve, to acquire, to learn, to experience. You can be grateful for the fact that there is time, because you can grow; but time is a two-edged sword. It gives you opportunities, but—especially as you grow older—time is no longer your friend. Time is shrinking."

The horizontal path, Tolle says, crosses our vertical path. It is made up of our ego, character defects, fears and desires to control: to sum this up—our messy humanness. It is this very suffering that can also bring awareness and growth: "You can see that the seemingly bad things in your life have a purpose, too," Tolle says. "They have brought you to the point of awakening."

With this awakening, Tolle says, suffering is "no longer compulsory. It is optional." Yes, challenges continue to come, but they are no longer transformed into suffering. "The successful life," Tolle says, "is a conscious life."

If you are rooted in the "present moment of being," Tolle says, you are grounded in the vertical path. You experience the passage of time in a more detached way. You watch what comes and goes from a place of awareness, but you are rooted in the timeless dimension of consciousness. I have discovered that the power of the horizontal path lessens with age. Instead, my program of recovery allows me to live "on the vertical" longer and more often. I can get there by taking one deep, conscious breath followed by another. This practice ultimately leads me to love and compassion. It is here that I can be more aware and awake, rather than giving in to my ego, character defects, fears and desires to control.

BE GRATEFUL FOR WHATEVER COMES

Early in my life, I was given the gift of visualization, especially in business. If I dreamed about an idea, I could visualize it, put it into words and set to work making it happen. When I was introduced to recovery from addiction through the 12 Steps, my world of visualization and consciousness expanded dramatically and gave greater meaning to my *whole* life. Today, I live as much as I can on the vertical path that Eckhart Tolle describes. I have learned *not* to attach myself to a desired outcome, but to give more attention to the journey that I am taking now. I focus on being aware of my consciousness and how that flows into everything that I do and say.

Whoever said that "aging isn't for sissies" was right, but I believe we can also choose to age with grace and dignity by cultivating this consciousness. I am committed to not letting "the old man in," but when he does arrive, I will be grateful and accept whatever he brings to my "guest house" door.

THE GUEST HOUSE

Rumi, 13th Century Persian poet, scholar and mystic

"This being home is a guest house.
Every morning a new arrival.

A joy, a depression, a meanness,
some momentary awareness comes
as an unexpected visitor.

Welcome and entertain them all!
Even if they are a crowd of sorrows,
who violently sweep your house
empty of its furniture,
still treat each guest honorably.
He may be clearing you out
for some new delight.

The dark thought, the shame, the malice,
meet them at the door laughing,
and invite them in.

Be grateful for whatever comes,
because each has been sent
as a guide from beyond."

MY FIRST 40 YEARS: A PATH TO SELF-DESTRUCTION

People always told me how lucky I was to have a comfortable home in rural Ellsworth, Wisconsin, and wonderful parents. It was true. As a little boy, I could roam the neighborhood and hang around with my older bachelor-farmer neighbors. But as I matured, I started to feel uneasy and discontented. I discovered that food—specifically snacks and sugar—always helped me feel better.

My own dad struggled with depression and fear, as well as chronic back pain. He sometimes drank too much beer, he smoked four packs a day and, if he started eating sugar, he couldn't stop.

Many years later, I recognized my own ever-present fear, depression, alcohol addiction and my powerful attraction to sugar: my first "feel-good" drug.

I experienced the buzz, the euphoria, and the contentment of a "sugar high" early. It saved me. Sugar was the easiest way to escape fear and pain. I also discovered carbs, especially bread and chips, that offered the same high because they quickly converted to sugar in my body.

Many decades ago, American health researchers declared that too much sugar not only adds calories and raises the risk of obesity, but it also accelerates aging.

Growing up as a chubby farm boy who struggled in school made me feel insecure. I was the odd kid wearing bib overalls who felt "less than." I wasn't born with low self-esteem, but it developed. To feel better, I used sugar and junk food to change the way I felt.

Looking back, I also had a learning disability, probably what we call ADHD today, but decades ago there was no such diagnosis. In addition, because I was slow to develop physically, I was treated with hormone shots. At 14, I overheard my dad say in a hushed voice as we visited my doctor: "Is he going to be a man?"

What little self-esteem I had, plummeted.

THE CONS AND THE CRAVINGS

I looked forward to the Wisconsin county fairs because I could binge on sweets, pop and fried foods. At 10, I started entering a calf as a 4-H project, but I never really raised the calf: I borrowed one from our neighbor. I turned these annual three-day events into four days with no adult supervision and I ate as much as I wanted. Food was love for me.

In time, food would become my life-long enemy.

I got to know the carnies and I copied them. I learned how to be charming and manipulative. I spent my young adulthood refining those skills and using them to my advantage. In high school, I needed money to buy snacks loaded with sugar, beer, cigarettes and addictive, black-market diet pills that were originally prescribed by my doctor because I was overweight.

Even as a kid, I had an entrepreneurial instinct. Somehow I knew that making money was the answer to building a big life—or so I thought. I worked deals with high school classmates who were as sneaky as I was. One friend stole clothes from his father's department store and charged me 10 percent of the purchase price so I could turn around and sell them for a profit. I offered year-old Christmas Seals as a charity fundraiser and pocketed the income. I skipped my classes and averaged a D on my report cards. My teacher told me the plain truth, "Burton," she warned me, "you'll never get to first base."

After high school, I joined the Army Reserve for seven years. That career choice involved weekly meetings, two annual active duty sessions and a six-month duty commitment at Fort Leonard Wood, Missouri. After basic training, I volunteered to be a second cook in the mess hall. That position not only gave me access to all the snacks I needed, but it also gave me power: I could trade five pounds of coffee for a weekend pass from the First Sergeant.

In my late teens and early 20s, I was loaded with optimism and ambition. I worked hard and I saw risk as opportunity, not the danger of failure. Like many budding entrepreneurs, I would sooner defy norms than conform. I sold magazines and advertising for businesses. I sold tubeless tire repair kits. I wasn't choosy about what I hawked.

Later in my 20s, I opened my own gas station business and that led to an expanding network of multiple, self-service gasoline and convenience food stores, as well as several real estate developments. Today everyone offers self-service gasoline and goods, but I was the pioneer—the very *first* to create these stores.

It was the 1960s and, by that time in my budding entrepreneurial career, I had multiple addictions firing: alcohol, cigarettes, diet pills and my lifelong addiction to compulsive overeating.

SUPERFICIAL, SELF-CENTERED AND SCARED

Making money and promoting was easy for me, but personal relationships were always difficult. They could be unpredictable and harmful because I was superficial, self-centered and scared.

When my first marriage ended in divorce, I was 80 pounds overweight. I realized that I had to take control of my life, so I joined Weight Watchers (the only guy among 20 women) and I lost the pounds. I started to clean up my life. I let go of cigarettes and diet pills, but food and alcohol continued to be my ever-present companions. I could not control these addictions, but I attempted to manage them. For example, I would not eat sugar at lunch because—if I did—I would have to eat sugar the rest of the day to maintain my sugar high.

I would not use alcohol unless I was in a safe place because—once I started—I could not stop. In my mid-to late 30s, I added gambling to my addictions and traveling to Las Vegas on junkets once or twice monthly for long weekends. I wasn't so interested in gambling, but those trips gave me the chance to indulge in my two main addictions: food and alcohol.

LIFE CLOSES IN

At age 39, my life was closing in on me. I was living in three "boxes": I was a successful businessman, a loving father of three children *and* an addict abusing food and alcohol (my "lesser" addictions were caffeine, gambling and work).

I had to keep those three "life boxes" separate. I could not let the father or the businessman mix with the addict.

I tried to maintain a normal weight, but my compulsive overeating led to 10-pound gains or fasting to lose pounds. My life was out of control!

Meanwhile, my second marriage was unraveling. I met with a marriage counselor each week. I was totally "locked-up" and it was painful: I was scared of being honest. I could not share my feelings or admit my severe insecurities. My wife, Sybil, was pregnant and I wasn't even talking about *that*. Even my teenage children noticed.

I needed alcohol to achieve some version of normal… and that worried me.

When I told a friend that I thought I should stop drinking, he suggested meeting with Dr. George Mann, a Minneapolis therapist who later became a pioneer in alcoholism treatment. Meeting with Dr. Mann was the beginning of a dramatic change. I gave up drinking. With the absence of alcohol, I realized that I was using food the same way: to change the way I felt.

I finally had the awareness to speak more openly with my marriage therapist. Up until that time, all I could say was, "There is something wrong with me." Without alcohol clouding my thinking, I could be candid, "There is something more going on than my relationship with my wife. It has to do with the way I use food."

"I believe you Burt," my therapist said with a direct gaze, "I urge you to meet with a professional who specializes in compulsive overeating."

This was the first time I heard those words "compulsive overeating." It was 1980 and our society knew little about food addiction in those days.

I began to cry…and then I had hope for the first time.

I attended a weekend retreat focused on understanding compulsive behaviors. The "aftercare" was a 12-Step program patterned after Alcoholics Anonymous called Overeaters Anonymous (OA). I started attending weekly meetings of OA at age 40 and I haven't stopped since.

When I decided to get help in 1980, OA was still a small movement. Obesity had become a national problem because two in three adults were considered overweight or obese and the trend was getting worse. I understood the ever-present danger of food addiction because I needed food to live. For the rest of my life, I would live daily with the "enemy": food.

I knew I could not succeed on my own.

MY LIFE TRANSFORMED

With help, I embarked on an amazing transition:

Forty years of looking successful from the outside and living secretly with a lot of pain on the inside had to end. The second half of my life would begin with a two-year shift from my old and familiar addictions to a new and untried "clean life." This was my big leap of faith. Could it work?

I always thought that if I took complete charge of my life and asked for no help, things would turn out exactly the way I wanted them.

That did not happen.

Instead, I embraced the opposite: I had to give up being in charge so that the gifts of abstinence *and* peace of mind could enter my life. All of my progress toward sanity and balance came from this one life-changing decision to practice the 12 Steps of OA. These OA Steps mirror the many 12-Step programs that have saved countless, addicted people around the world from illness and premature death.

When I let go of using food and alcohol to maintain my compulsive, out-of-control life, I had to let go of friends who ate and drank like I did. I realize now that those friendships were based on our shared addictions and little else. What *did* last were my business relationships that were made of stronger stuff.

When I discovered real recovery, I turned my life and my will over to the care of God as I understood God. The 12th Step of recovery asks each of us, who have experienced a "spiritual awakening" as a result of adopting this new way of living, to carry the message of hope to others who still struggle.

Addiction is a disease, although too many people privately call these dangerous behaviors with drugs, alcohol, food, sex, spending, porn—you name it—a moral failing. The American Society of Addiction Medicine (ASAM) calls addiction a disease and describes it this way: "a chronic, relapsing brain disorder characterized by compulsive seeking and use despite harmful consequences."

Here is the hard truth: addiction leads many of us to hurtful, harmful, even life-threatening decisions and actions. When we are deep in our disease, our moral compass has no true north.

A LIFESAVING IDEA

The 12th Step of my recovery program asks me to tell others that recovery *is* possible, and serve as a willing source of help to people who are still deep in their disease. This is where service comes in. For most of us in recovery, service comes naturally: we are so grateful to get our lives back that we offer support to others eagerly.

An ambitious idea surfaced around 2008 for me: I decided to write an autobiography. I wanted to share the story of what I had experienced in my first 70 years and honestly describe how food addiction and alcoholism had colored every corner of my life. My book—intended largely for my family—was called *Living With The Enemy* and the project gave me the gift of intense self-reflection. I later realized that more people than my family might benefit from my story.

A book about compulsive overeating authored by a man was an anomaly nearly two decades ago. Women were far more willing to talk about their food issues. It wasn't until 2017 that the American Psychiatric Association even added "Food Addiction" to their mental illness "bible": the DSM-5 (Diagnostic and Statistical Manual of Mental Disorders).

In my deepest addictive place, I hid my disease. I still had the "look good" working for me and so do a lot of people who only binge in private. How do we do it? We exercise excessively. We starve ourselves to compensate. We lie to ourselves and make countless promises to change our pattern "tomorrow" or, at the very latest, next week. We break those promises repeatedly.

Lifting the veil on my own addiction and telling my story took some courage, but I wanted to help people more than I wanted to protect my image. I decided to tell the whole truth.

Living With The Enemy was published in 2010, it was well-received and won a Midwest Book Award. I wondered: maybe I can do more?

That is when COR retreat (Latin for heart) was born in Wayzata, a suburb of Minneapolis, Minnesota (www.cormn.org). I wanted to create a retreat like the one that helped me, only better: more focused, affordable and funded for the long term. I wanted to create a program that was not at the whim of insurers: a reality that is still sadly true today.

Like all things in my business life, COR started with a vision. I described my idea to several close friends, especially Tim and Steve, my wise recovery sponsors and dear friends in OA. They would later become COR volunteers. I told them this:

"I want to design and fund a residential, non-profit, 12-Step focused retreat center for people struggling with food addiction. I want it to be affordable, not like those 30-day residential programs that cost as much as $40,000. I want this retreat to teach people how to live happily and healthfully with a workable food plan, how to turn their addiction over to a Higher Power, and how to be accountable and supported by other people on the same recovery path. When our guests leave COR, we will suggest that their "aftercare" be OA. We will help as many people as possible and if someone can't pay for our very affordable program, they can apply for a partial scholarship."

It all came together: the location at the McIver Center at The Retreat (a center for treating alcohol and drug addiction) in Wayzata, Minnesota, the curriculum for a five-day, residential program, the staff, and our army of volunteers (25 in all) who make our program work.

Our first leader, Michelle, and later, Nancy—both women with long personal recovery from food addiction, as well as extensive experience as educators—became our wise facilitators. Nancy attended COR and lost 100 pounds safely. Today, in her role as Executive Director and leader of COR, Nancy is essential to our organization's growth and stability. Her commitment helps our successful program continue to thrive and help save lives.

Scott, my nephew (also in recovery) and I created the original recovery program plan, guided by our own experience with food addiction. Kathy, my assistant, and Gail, my sister and longtime business partner, were right there from the beginning offering support. All we needed were people to join us for our first retreat in August, 2011.

IF YOU BUILD IT, THEY WILL COME

One more miracle: I was invited to appear on a popular Twin Cities TV news program and had two minutes to tell my story and describe COR Retreat. Within a few days, we had our first group of 14 guests joining us. Since then, more than 2,300 people have attended COR retreats. There is no other residential treatment center like ours addressing food addiction in the United States. People join us from all over the world.

COR Retreat is a five-day, four-night experience. Participants openly share their struggles with food and compulsive overeating, often for the first time. During their stay, our guests are introduced to physical recovery from compulsive overeating, emotional recovery and spiritual healing: all three are vital components of lasting good health.

Practical tools of recovery, successful eating plans (including a definition of what constitutes "clean food"), the importance of supportive relationships, what spiritual health means, and identifying community support resources are all part of the COR program.

In our safe and confidential retreat setting, attendees learn to practice the first three steps of their 12-Step recovery program: 1. They come to believe that, on their own, they are powerless over their own food choices, 2. They realize that a Power greater than themselves (their own definition) can restore them to sane eating, and 3. They decide to turn their lives and will over to the care of this healing Power, so they can sustain a healthy food program for life. This third step includes participation in regular recovery meetings with their peers, working with a personal sponsor who is experienced in the program and offering hope to others who struggle as they do.

Since COR's founding in 2011, I visit our retreats often and tell my story to our Encore group whose members have embraced the first three Steps of recovery from food addiction and practice the OA Steps 4-12 regularly.

These Steps require each person to:

- Examine every choice and behavior involving food,
- Conduct a fearless moral inventory of hurtful behavior in all aspects of life,
- Make appropriate amends to people they have hurt,
- Seek frequent guidance from their Higher Power or God of their understanding, and
- Carry the message of recovery and offer support to others who struggle with compulsive overeating.

This recovery program requires honesty, commitment and consistency, but if all three are present, the outcomes are life-changing and life-saving.

EXPERIENCE, STRENGTH AND HOPE

We are told in addiction recovery circles that if we want to keep our sobriety, we have to give it away. The best way to maintain my own healthy recovery is to share my story with our COR guests. I am sharing my story more than ever and I notice that the experience enriches my emotional resilience and connection with like-minded people in ways I never imagined—especially at this advanced age when some of us see our lives becoming limited and smaller.

People in recovery stay engaged because they're giving back. It's the opposite of becoming irrelevant. I love the questions and insights that flow from these conversations that come from our COR guests when I share my story. Here is a glimpse:

How long will it be before I feel comfortable around food?

Please let go of this expectation. Plan on living your program just one day at a time. Twenty four hours is achievable. That is enough. All those days will add up to many years. In 2025, I marked 47 years.

Is abstinence still important to you at 87?

Yes, even at my advanced age! Food is different from alcohol or a drug because we have to eat. Even after all these years, I need my daily plan. Here's the difference: if you're visualizing perfect abstinence with alcohol, imagine a bowling ball going straight down the middle of a highway. But with food, you have to eat. You will drift from one side of the highway to the other with your food choices and you will have to make corrections. I still take this zigzag path at times. I know I have to live within my food plan for the rest of my life. I make corrections and learn as I go. I stay away from binge foods. To me, these are salty, crunchy, sweet or fatty. I call them "exciting foods." If I start eating any of them, I cannot stop. If I stop, I may not be able to stay stopped, even after all these years of abstinence practice. If

I indulge, I feel bad. In order to be happy, joyous and free, I have to stick to my "clean eating."

Recovery gave me this: I am no longer uncomfortable around these "exciting" foods. Nor do I have to "white knuckle" it. I don't want to eat anything that will endanger me. I still write my plan down daily and I often share that plan with my sponsor. I no longer weigh and measure my food because I have enough experience with what I am seeing to be accurate. My food plan is healthy and desirable.

What can you suggest that will help me not "drive off the road"?

To continue and help ensure my recovery all these years, I had to do these important things:

- I had to give the story of my recovery away and help others to see what is possible. Telling my story is a lifesaver for me. Founding COR was my commitment to these goals.
- Staying in touch with my "fellow travelers" in person, on Zoom, FaceTime and on the phone has been vital. I do it daily.
- Meeting regularly with my OA sponsors is a must.

What more will make a positive difference for people like you and me?

Along with having a food plan, practicing clean eating, going to meetings and staying in close touch with your OA sponsor, make time for healthy exercise and exploring your faith. If you were raised in a faith tradition and you left it behind, revisit it. If a tradition appeals to you, explore it. Staying "spiritually fit" will enrich your program of recovery and make you stronger than ever. Also, ask your sponsor or recovery friends for ideas that worked for them in early recovery.

Will COR always be available?

We have created a foundation to ensure that COR will continue for a long, long time and provide scholarships when people need financial help. Our non-profit foundation pays approximately half of all our operating costs.

Are you happy with how COR has evolved?

When I think about my life legacy, I think of my family and our three generations living honest, healthy, and contributing lives. I think of the wealth that my entrepreneurial life has produced. I think of COR and its success in helping people address and live safely with the disease of addiction. On the scale of importance, COR is second only to my family.

RECOVERY AND AGING

Recovery saved my life…and extended it. Adopting the 12 Steps and applying them daily has been—and continues to be—the most important life choice I have ever taken. I did not make this decision alone. I relied on the 12 Steps and my faith to address my two addictions that were bound to kill me: compulsive overeating and alcoholism. Today, I rely on the 12 Steps as much as ever, or more so, as I face the inevitable life changes of aging.

On page 109, you will find all 12 Steps in their original language written 90 years ago. I'll describe the first three Steps in a simple, declarative, 10-word "shorthand" that people like me use:

"I can't, God can; I think I'll let Him."

Steps 4 through 12 continue:

They require me to take a full look at my life (a "searching and fearless moral inventory"), share that inventory out loud with someone I trust, make amends to the people I have hurt, continue to monitor my daily decisions and actions, admit when I'm wrong, ask God (as I understand God) to give me the power to pay attention to what is right, practice these 12-Step principles in all my affairs, and finally, share these Steps for living in service to others who are struggling with addiction.

This is my recovery *and* my aging program. Living this way isn't easy, but I have found nothing more authentic and enduring than this guidance for a good and honest life. Practicing the 12 Steps requires no religious affiliation, no political persuasion, no public declaration, no financial investment, no promotion.

You can use these Steps no matter what your personal circumstances may be. Review the Steps as they were first written and you will see that only the First Step names "alcohol": "We admitted we were powerless over alcohol—that our lives had become unmanageable."

Now delete the word "alcohol" and insert whatever you are powerless over (all of us can name at least one thing). If you can't think of a single thing, insert "aging."

If we live long enough, we will be powerless over some aspects of our aging. Today, I rely on 12-Step wisdom to embrace aging, instead of fighting it. In doing so, I'm making the most of my final life chapter. I will share what I have learned and practiced in the hope that you will find what I say useful. I will focus on these five, universal topics as we age:

- The Art of Acceptance,
- Emotional Resilience and Connection,
- Struggles and Suffering,
- What it Means to Be Happy, Joyous and Free,
- Approaching Death

THE ART OF ACCEPTANCE

My 12-Step program has allowed me to live a life that is more balanced, serene, aware and awake. I have come to believe that everything (yes, everything) that has happened in my life was not an accident or coincidence.

Each event is God acting anonymously in my life.

The serenity prayer, written in the 1930s by Protestant theologian Reinhold Niebuhr, has helped me accept the unexpected and the unbidden:

> *"God, grant me the serenity to accept the things I cannot change; courage to change the things I can; and wisdom to know the difference.*
> *Living one day at a time; Enjoying one moment at a time;*
> *Accepting hardships as the pathway to peace;*
> *Taking, as He did, this sinful world as it is, not as I would have it;*
> *Trusting that He will make things right if I surrender to His Will so that I may be reasonably happy in this life,*
> *And be supremely happy with Him forever and ever in the next.*
> *Amen."*

One of the best parts of living into my 80s is participating in the lives of our family which numbers 26 including 5 adult children, 12 grandchildren, 7 spouses, my wife of 35 years, Yvonne, and me. I have often wondered if Steps One, Two and Three of the 12 Steps were created expressly for parents and grandparents!

It's tough to realize that your span of control legally ends when a child reaches eighteen.

For a person like me whose first thought is always to take control, my recovery program has helped me stand back, take a deep breath, and not say the first thing that comes to my mind. I know that I cannot be at the center of my adult children's lives. At best, my wife Yvonne and I are loving witnesses and helpmates when we are asked to be.

LOVING FIERCELY

Recovery has taught me about boundaries—a concept totally foreign to me in my younger years. Now I know where I begin and end and where the people I love begin and end. I continue to practice staying on my side of that boundary line. Sure, I sometimes stub my toe on the line, but I learn more every time I do.

I love fiercely. As long as I live, I will worry about some of the choices that my adult children and grandchildren make, but each of them must live their own lives. My recovery has introduced me to deep-down acceptance of this singular fact. With genuine acceptance (not the lip service kind), I worry less and love my children and grandchildren a lot more, especially when they struggle.

With time, I have come to understand the wisdom of acceptance in parenting and grandparenting. It is not about giving in, as I first thought. It is about living life on life's terms. Seeing reality. Knowing where I begin and end. Knowing where my control and influence ends.

This is one of my favorite passages from the Big Book of Alcoholics Anonymous. You don't have to be in recovery from addiction to find this helpful in your life. It's my "compass" for relationships of every kind and it is vital to life with my adult children and grandchildren:

"And acceptance is the answer to *all* my problems today. When I am disturbed, it is because I find some person, place, thing or situation—some fact of my life—unacceptable to me and I can find no serenity until I accept that person, place, thing or situation as being exactly the way it is supposed to be at this moment. Nothing, absolutely nothing, happens in God's world by mistake. Until I could accept my alcoholism, I could not stay sober; unless I accept life completely on life's terms, I cannot be happy. I need to concentrate not so much on what needs to be changed in the world as on what needs to be changed in me and in my attitudes."

GOOD ORDERLY DIRECTION

I am blessed with a cadre of loving, genuine friends. I would not have these solid relationships without recovery: I would be dead already or an angry, isolated old man who is still drinking, drugging and overeating. I am none of these things, but I *am* facing the inevitable losses of aging.

I can choose to accept life on life's terms, including going blind from glaucoma. I have learned that acceptance is the answer to all my problems today including my continuing loss of eyesight and these additional physical maladies: prostate cancer successfully treated in 2008, a heart condition that required a pacemaker in 2021, a case of Long COVID, and occasional dizziness and intermittent trouble walking.

When these realities began to appear, I leaned heavily on the first three steps of my 12-Step program:

I am powerless over my physical condition, I believe that a power greater than myself will restore me to sanity as I navigate these health issues, *and* I can make a daily decision to turn this cavalcade of conditions over to God as I understand God and seek instruction. I call this Good Orderly Direction.

I do none of this alone. I look forward to my weekly 12-Step meetings and I rely on several sponsors who have also become close friends. These friends are aware and awake and practicing active recovery. We talk daily and share openly about our lives and the recovery steps that guide us. Acceptance and honesty are common denominators of our sharing, especially as we age.

DO NOT GIVE UP ON LIFE

At 83 ½ in 2021, I was hiking and mountain road biking up 14,000-foot peaks in Colorado and downhill skiing on Vail Mountain with my wife, Yvonne.

A couple years earlier in 2019 we had planned a circumnavigation of the world aboard our sailboat *Serenity 2*.

Then the world as we knew it stopped.

An acute respiratory syndrome called coronavirus 2 appeared for the first time in Wuhan, China in December, 2019. Soon, the virus spread to other areas of Asia and in January, 2020, the World Health Organization declared a worldwide public health emergency. By March, 2020 the outbreak was an official pandemic called COVID-19.

Our plans for a circumnavigation came to a screeching halt. By the grace of God, we had not started our global sailing trip, so we safely "sheltered in place" at our condo home in Florida and sailed *Serenity 2* in the waters off the U.S. Virgin Islands. Long distance sailors who had ventured out before the pandemic, were stranded on islands in the South Pacific and they could not leave or enter other countries for two years.

By January 2021, Yvonne and I made a major decision: we sold *Serenity 2* after our final sailing trip in May, 2021 and we closed on the purchase of our new beach home in Venice, Florida, in the spring. A nine-month remodeling project began.

Serenity 2 and her predecessors brought us immense joy for more than 40 years. To a serious sailor, our aquatic crafts are truly living beings. Letting them go is like watching our loved humans depart. If we are fortunate enough to grow old, aging offers an opportunity to acknowledge that everything we've worked so hard for—our relationships, our possessions, our accomplishments—will eventually leave us or be left behind.

MY SPORTS, MY PASSIONS

In June, 2021, I was diagnosed with orthostatic hypertension. My blood pressure dropped to 75/50 and my pulse at rest was 38. I was 83 ½ when the doctors at the Mayo Clinic in Florida implanted a pacemaker. Shortly thereafter, I was diagnosed with Long COVID. I'm not exactly sure which came first: the low blood pressure or the Long COVID and both may have been COVID-related. This disease is a mystery and doctors still don't have a good handle on the symptoms. Because of these combined health issues, I had to let go of my favorite sports.

There were days when I could not walk a block without being exhausted for two days. I was often too dizzy or unstable to even walk to the beach in front of our home. My days had a familiar pattern: wake up, feel fairly normal, do my 15-minute morning Pilates exercise and, within an hour, I would be too dizzy to stand. Lay down and rest for two to three hours, or even a full day. As long as I remained on the couch, I could manage.

My glaucoma, diagnosed nearly 13 years before, was also advancing steadily.

Only six months earlier at 83, I could hike up a 14,000-foot mountain trail in Vail, ski the demanding Colorado "14ers" or bike up Mount Evans, a 14,500-foot peak. Long COVID and orthostatic hypertension made pursuing my favorite mountain sports and sailing the oceans no longer attainable.

ACCEPTANCE IS THE ANSWER

Meanwhile, my mind and heart were at odds. My active life was always a benchmark on my journey toward aging. My mind told me, "You can still do it!" but my body said, "No! You cannot." It was a powerful argument waged in my mind because these sports were integral to my very identity.

I had to face a new reality: I struggled with both mountain altitude and poor vision, but living in paradise on the Florida coast made this new limited lifestyle a gift, not a loss. We moved into our newly-remodeled beach home in June, 2023 and I was much happier (and safer) at sea level than in the mountains.

Yvonne and I still traveled to visit our other homes and our children and grandchildren. It seemed, as long as I had an arm to hold onto or a bench nearby, I could manage. This went on for nearly two years and, by the time my health returned to normal (or close to normal), I was 85 ½ years old.

But age caught up with me.

Had I still been ruled by my addictions, alcohol and food, I would have been helpless, hopeless and hell-on-wheels for everyone close to me. The guidance of my friends in recovery and the 12 Steps gave me a life-saving faith and enduring acceptance that have proven themselves countless times when I indulged in abject fear and "poor me" resistance.

I have learned to practice acceptance like my life depends on it…because it does. Rather than mourning those losses of my favorite sports, I have embraced new ways to find joy: practicing my Pilates and stretching every morning, exercising in the pool, walking on the beach or taking a walk into town while listening to podcasts. These activities don't offer the same thrill as skiing, hiking or riding my road bike up Mount Evans, but they offer me their own welcomed peace today.

STAY ENGAGED, GIVE BACK

Because of good genes, a little bit of luck and excellent health care, my low blood pressure returned to normal and I recovered from Long COVID. Thanks to my recovery program, I let go of my favorite sports with God-given grace, rather than being embittered and nursing the blues.

When I turned 84, I recall asking my internist why I was still going strong with my favorite sports at 83 and then things radically changed. I saw this in my friends, too. We were all doing less and slowing down. We welcomed naps in the afternoon. We also recognized that we had become less relevant to modern life as it sped past us. Some of us became less engaged in life.

My physician's answer to my query about all these changes was unadorned: "Burt, it's simply aging," he said. Oh.

I left my doctor's office with a declaration: slowing down is one thing, but stopping is another. I will not stop. Yes, it is easy to do nothing much in retirement, but it is healthier to keep *doing*. My recovery program helps me in two ways: giving back by supporting others who struggle with our shared addictions, and second, attending 12-Step meetings with my peers in person or on Zoom and FaceTime. Both pay big dividends with camaraderie, honest sharing and fellowship.

Please keep in mind that the wisdom of the 12 Steps can apply to more than addiction. These Steps can help any one of us cope with the challenges and changes of aging.

EMBRACE GRATITUDE

I have new limitations to face. I cannot drive because I have about 20 percent vision remaining. My world view is definitely fuzzy and gray, but not dark. Still, I remain truly grateful and sustained by my 12-Step program and daily conversations with my supportive "fellow travelers" and trusted friends.

I have been able to see for 87 years and watch my grandchildren grow up. I can still see the sun slowly sink into the ocean. I am neither fearful of going blind nor afraid of death. Once we experience awareness and the God of our understanding in our daily life, this understanding offers relief from the pain, fear, loss, anger and other difficulties that come with aging. How? Every time I have an unrealistic fear or when I'm depressed, I remember the Guest House poem (page 11) with an excerpt here. It gives me perspective:

> *"A joy, a depression, a meanness…Welcome and entertain them all!…the dark thought, the shame, the malice, meet them at the door laughing, and invite them in. Be grateful for whatever comes, because each has been sent as a guide from beyond."*

If I'm entertaining my fear of dying, I say "Welcome. Come on in, let's sit down and talk." Eventually, I hope to enter into union with the Divine. I believe that all our souls transcend death and we are either reincarnated or changed into some other form that joins the God of our understanding.

One good thing about having glaucoma and going blind is that I can accept my aging body with more dignity and good humor because I don't see the world very well! I tell my wife that she is more beautiful than ever and Yvonne reminds me that she is grateful for my limited eyesight.

I live my life, to the best of my ability, on the "vertical path" that philosopher and spiritual teacher Eckhart Tolle talks about: I was born happy. I hope to die happy and be with the God of my understanding. The distractions of the "horizontal path" made up of my ego, defects, fears and desires, have lessened with age.

I am grateful.

THE GRACE OF ACCEPTANCE

No longer participating in athletic activities has been difficult, but I have not given up on life. I am practicing acceptance, adaptation and trust so I can age with grace, with God's help.

For most of the year, Yvonne and I live in our beautiful Gulfside home in Florida where I can comfortably move around. I enjoy the sunshine in my hammock on our outside deck, I swim in our pool and still walk a good distance daily or, if I'm not up to it, just a few yards to the white, sand beach. We have our homes in Vail and St. Paul, Minnesota, where we are able to get out of the hot Florida summers, and keep up with the lives of our adult children and grandchildren. We are blessed indeed.

TURNING IT OVER...

Starting my estate planning more than 30 years ago was another act of acceptance and letting go. I began this work with my brother Ron and my friend and professional estate planner, Jeff Teggler. Jeff knows the estate rules and regulations fully and, with additional professional help, we established trust funds for our five adult children. Ron became my full-time estate and investment advisor until his death in 2019 and Jeff continued as a vital advisor as Yvonne and I decided to give more than 50 percent of my net worth to our family.

This process isn't just about financial planning alone. The decisions I'm making ensure that my adult children and my grandchildren will be secure and prepared for their futures. This gives me immense gratification.

I have also engaged Casey Richter to work with my family as the lead trustee of my estate along with Bill

Wanner, my long-time real estate partner and a member of the family office of Cresset/Meristem. They make all the financial distribution decisions and investment decisions. Not me.

...AND THEN SOME

Another aspect of acceptance and letting go is recognizing that work and making money are no longer the most important things in my life. At this stage, I'm often surprised when I reflect on the successes I've had in business. I am pleased that I can provide financial security for all my children and grandchildren.

Today, however, my earning power and net worth is not the measure of me. I still do some business consulting, but I no longer make big business decisions. I don't even follow business news or the stock market regularly. The market is one more thing I don't have control over; I try not to let the intense machinations affect me.

I find my new attitude about this facet of my financial life refreshing and freeing.

When I sold the business that I started 57 years earlier at age 30, you might think that giving that up was a struggle. It was not. But aren't all successful entrepreneurs control freaks? Not this one. From the start-up of my first Auto Stop "gas and goods" station (later called SSG Corporation), I was an expert at delegating responsibility. I was the one who envisioned the business, put together a successful model and delegated the rest to totally reliable people who I hired.

My role at SSG was largely deciding where the next store would be located and my sister, Gail, and our staff did all the rest. I was never the hands-on person. Frankly, I'm a bit lazy. I didn't go to the office until about 10 a.m. most days. I was not the classic "driven entrepreneur" nor did I identify with that life. It is true that people like me who are addicts thrive on being in control, but my control in business was different. Rather than controlling the whole company, all I controlled was how and what I delegated to others. When I found recovery from addiction, I learned even more about conscious acceptance and letting go. This new way of thinking has enriched my physical, mental and spiritual well-being dramatically.

I was actually relieved when I sold SSG because my identity never was interwoven with the enterprise. Thanks to my program of recovery, I never felt compelled to know about or weigh-in on every aspect of my company because I had a beautiful recovery life outside of SSG. Selling my company was winning in my estimation, because that's when I received my financial reward.

Now at 87, I honestly do not feel the need to control anything.

Married January 4, 1992 in Vail, Colorado

Burt, Dad, Grandpa

Burt and Yvonne with Chase

Jennie and Jane

left to right:
Michael, Gabe, Nicholas, Samuel, Isaac

Nick and Becky,
married July, 2021

Sam and Chloe,
married October, 2026

Michael

Isaac

Gabe

John and Tammy

left to right:
Sonny, John, Tammy, Seth, Samara

Samara

Seth

Sonny

Anne and Aaron,
married August, 2025

Anne and Aaron's family
left to right: Joel, Les, Anne, Aaron, Gillian, Sofia

Les

Joel

Les and Joel

Katie and Rob

left to right:
Jack, Katie, Murphy, Rob

Murphy and Jack

Brian and Jordan,
married April, 2025

Serenity 2, sold 2021

Our forever home – Venice, Florida

Life is good: aging with grace

Moon over Vail Mountain

NOT LOSS, BUT GAINS

Accepting change and letting go is one of the hardest lessons that aging teaches us. Whether it's letting go of possessions, work or activities we once loved, if we have given any of these things too much power, we can feel like we're losing pieces of ourselves.

I have learned that letting go is not about loss; instead, it is about making space for what truly matters *now*. It helps me shed what no longer serves me, making room for what brings me joy: meaning and connection *today*. Whether it is letting go of possessions or releasing the desire to take on more business projects, I'm discovering that "decluttering my life" gives me a greater sense of freedom and control.

By simplifying our living spaces and mental landscapes, we can create environments that truly support our well-being and independence. Decluttering—whether physical, mental or financial—is a powerful practice as we age because this is a time when clarity of purpose and comfort become even more essential. My wife, Yvonne, has mastered the art of decluttering and, for us, it is liberating.

When we declutter, we do more than simply lighten our load and re-organize our homes. We create space for new experiences, relationships and personal growth. This decision allows us to redefine our identities at this life stage and focus on our *current* values and priorities. This step is a powerful form of renewal that is both energizing and inspiring.

Yvonne and I have accumulated countless belongings and each item can be tied to memories and often a purposeful endeavor: from clothes we no longer wear to furniture gathering dust in storage to keepsakes that remind us of memorable times. These belongings can become a burden more than a blessing. We are grateful for what we have and we have no desire to accumulate any more. We're also pleased that our adult children are enjoying the art and furniture that we have gifted to them.

These three ideas can help anyone "declutter with purpose"—1. Start early: do not wait until the assignment becomes overwhelming, 2. Involve family members in decisions about sentimental items, 3. View downsizing as an opportunity to simplify and prioritize.

Decluttering isn't just about creating physical space: it is about clearing mental space. I have learned that a simpler environment allows me to focus on what truly brings joy: my family, the health I *still* have and meaningful experiences and projects *right now*. When our spaces are cluttered, it can feel as though our possessions (or our worries about them) are controlling us. When my end of life comes, I aim to have my belongings reduced to a single banker's box.

I am grateful for our home in Florida and I have no desire for anything bigger or better. We have also added a 900-square-foot, second home in a new senior living compound called Marvella in Highland Park, St. Paul. This area was our neighborhood many decades ago. Returning gives Yvonne and I treasured in-person time with our adult children and grandchildren who live nearby and it relieves us of the hot Florida summers.

Never mind that our four suitcases seemed to fill the entire space at Marvella when we arrived! This change in lifestyle took some adaptation, but consider what we gained: seeing our adult children and grandchildren often, reconnecting with old friends, and making the most of Marvella's gym, sauna, hot tub, swimming pool and an easy walk to the mighty Mississippi River that runs through our capitol city, St. Paul, Minnesota.

Everybody at Marvella is old, like us, although Yvonne is 10 years my junior. We're accustomed to being around a variety of ages in Florida, so this dominant senior demographic requires some adjustment. If I dare compare myself to others, I think my view is distorted. I'm probably one of the most senior residents at 87, even though I like to *think* that I don't look my age. Don't we all tell ourselves that?

EMOTIONAL RESILIENCE AND CONNECTION

In our American society, we become less relevant as we age and that is a hard reality to face especially for men (myself included) who have enjoyed power, wealth and influence. Some friends and acquaintances don't like hearing this, but others quietly acknowledge that irrelevance is the unspoken fact of aging.

Look around you. Younger people are making the decisions—big and small.

When I shared this notion with other men—some five or ten years younger than myself—they were surprised. The mental image of grandpa in a wheelchair with a blanket on his lap—if it's you—can be arresting. Some said they never imagined becoming less relevant but by talking openly about it, the resistance diminishes and emotional resilience takes its place. We find the grace to accept our new status.

Seeing reality clearly with rigorous honesty is fundamental to aging. Let's be willing to let others do things for us: make the reservations, organize the trips, drive the car, plan the future. And let's be gracious about it. Resistance only creates suffering, but acceptance brings peace.

MORE 'BEING' – LESS 'DOING'

One way or another, as we age, we learn to relinquish control. There were times during my bout with Long COVID that I had trouble simply walking. During that time, I carved out time to get closer to the God of my understanding. I started meditating, practiced deep breathing and learned to spend more time in the present moment. Let's face it. This behavior is foreign to the hard-charging business owner that I once was. Selfishness is deeply ingrained in all of us and letting go of "self" demands surrender.

I have discovered this surrender in meditation. For me, the ancient practice is a prayer of quiet and a prayer of my heart. My ego is not present during meditation and, when my ego inevitably re-asserts itself, I let it pass and return to prayer in that quiet space with God. This new practice has awakened my happiness, contentment, fulfillment and gratitude. I am noticing that I can embody spontaneous kindness, both for myself and for others. As I age, I am learning to surrender and live more fully in that space that Eckhart Tolle calls the "vertical path."

I believe that surrender has positioned me to begin moving beyond this life as I know it with courage, joy and happiness. Surrender means turning my life and my will over to the care of God as I understand God. It means letting go of ego. God was present when I decided to get clean with food and abstinent from alcohol. My trust in

God will lead me to the end of my life. I am practicing this acceptance and surrender through meditation.

When we come to the end, I believe we will need to accept and surrender. Wouldn't it make sense to prepare in advance?

'FELLOW TRAVELERS': MY POSSE

These days, I stay in close touch daily with my friends who I call "fellow travelers." We connect by phone or FaceTime and we read from the "Big Book" of Alcoholics Anonymous plus the writings of Eckhart Tolle and American spiritual leader Ram Dass. I smile as I reflect on this new life that I have adopted: it is so far removed from my all-consuming business life, the extreme sports and, frankly, the extreme-everything that I embraced in my self-centered pre-recovery life.

Daily, I talk with Tim, Bob and Steve, my recovery program co-sponsors. All three men are, in Tolle's definition, "aware and awake." I have other friends who are not "working a program" (as we call it in recovery circles) but they are equally invested in speaking and sharing honestly and openly on a deeper level than many men won't or can't. This candor isn't the norm in our society and it is especially uncomfortable for men in their later years.

I'm convinced that the best way we can age with grace is to live in the here and now. That means focusing on *being* because most of us are done with our relentless *doing*.

We have considerable wisdom to share if we take the time to explore all that we have experienced and learned. If ever there was a time for deep connection, it is in this advancing age. We have the benefit of the long view and we can be witnesses to the scars, struggles and triumphs that shaped us. We are ready to be more candid and fearless than we have ever been.

SACRED 'CONNECTIVE TISSUE'

Intimate conversations with other men—especially as we age—feels like unearthing a rare treasure. Why? Our society tends to prioritize the arc of a life story far more than the rich, emotional nuances embedded within that story. A small circle of my trusted peers have become a safe sanctuary for us to go deep, share our stories, allow ourselves to be vulnerable and learn from our self-reflection. This is a gift I never imagined possible decades ago.

As a seasoned man in his 80s, an undeniable shift has occurred. At this stage, I am realizing that a man's desire for authenticity begins to outweigh his need for the "look good" of pretense. Opening the door to intimate conversation means encouraging each other to lower our guard and move past surface-level exchanges about achievements or regrets. It means digging deep into the subterranean terrain of feeling. Let's be frank: women naturally understand and embrace this practice, but men have to dare to go there.

In these moments of sharing, even this simple question "*How are you, really?*" can open the floodgates to revelations about fear, insecurity, hope and longing. I've experienced this in my sailboat cockpit, in my living room, on FaceTime and in Zoom meetings. These are not the tidy narratives that society seems to prefer: instead, we witness rare candor. This sharing is often messy, textured and raw with the emotional layers that shape—and sometimes reshape—our relationships with each other and ourselves.

As people age, I also notice that some lives get narrow and narrower because some of us don't have the connections we once had. To counteract that, I am focusing on never losing touch. That means reaching out to people of all ages (including my grandchildren) and paying attention to what is going on in their lives...not just my own. Yes, this takes initiative, but it yields richness and genuine gratitude.

When we address our aging and share our experiences honestly, we are creating a powerful "connective tissue" among our peers and family. When we speak as older men about our evolving bodies, our shifting priorities, our failing memories and our mortality, our stories are less about the details of what happened and more about what it really feels like for us. Speaking this openly takes courage, but the rewards of insight, shared understanding and support are worth it.

When sponsors from a 12-Step program are part of the discussion, the sharing goes deeper still. Here is why: our addiction recovery journeys teach us the value of honesty and emotional exposure. This was required if we were to find lasting recovery, so this practice naturally spills over into our personal conversations with other men (and women). Our talks are not founded merely on camaraderie, but on accountability, compassion and the willingness to witness and respect another person's interior world.

Scary at first? Yes, it can be. By consistently inviting and modeling this vulnerability, I have seen those stereotypical male barriers dissolve and conversations begin to echo with real understanding—sometimes marked by laughter, sometimes bathed in silence and often heavy with emotion. These dialogues remind me that personal storytelling, at its deepest, is not just the recounting of events, but the sharing of our hearts, our doubts and our hopes for redemption. This is where I find awakening, awareness and trust for each of us.

GOD IS A LOCAL CALL

These deeper conversations that mean so much today, actually started decades ago when I bought my first ocean-going sailboat in 1980. Now, more than 50 years later, they continue on land.

In my early days of sailing with my family and friends, we routinely "unplugged" all the electronics aboard our sailboat in order to appreciate the beauty of nature and the peace of living on the water far away from our bustling "land lives."

Sailing always gave me rich insights that I didn't readily realize in my day-to-day land life. On the water, there are fewer distractions by far and there is time to be contemplative. I gave myself permission to simply *be* rather than always *do*. On the ocean, I told my friends and family that God was a local call.

I took yearly sailing trips with my male friends beginning in 2002. There were plenty of hijinks, colorful stories and fun on those one to two-week trips, but something else happened when we got together in the cockpit each morning with coffee. We shared levels of honesty, openness, willingness and trust that are not usually associated with the males of our species.

The tradition started with my wife, Yvonne, when we sailed our boat alone. We each chose a morning reading from a favorite book. As the sun rose, we took time to reflect on the wise words that touched us most. We read them aloud to each other and our sharing was deep.

When I decided to host my guy friends on our sailboat, I suggested an early morning "cockpit conversation." No pressure. Listening was enough; sharing was optional. My favorite readings came from Alcoholics Anonymous and recovery books. For some of my sailing buddies, the 12 Steps were new concepts: they didn't struggle with addiction, but they had tough times and trials, even though they were highly successful by society's standards.

EVERYONE COMES WITH A LIMP

In the first five minutes in the cockpit, we got the small talk out of the way and the sharing got deep—fast. I saw my friends open up more and more with each day and they saw me do the same. The experience was life-changing and I witnessed genuine vulnerability and discovery on my friends' faces. In those cockpit conversations, our sharing eventually circled around to gratitude.

If our cockpit experience was so magical, I thought, why not replicate it in the Colorado Rockies during our biking and hiking adventures? That was the start of our Mindful Mens' Cycling: a biking, meditation and yoga weekend involving about eight or ten of us. In our group sharing, we used the Socratic method based on first asking questions to stimulate thought and then inviting sharing. One of our "young pups," who was only in his 50s, told us he was amazed: "Nobody puts on a costume. Nobody is faking," he said. "These are Type A guys but they have left that world behind. The only Type A part was the group's insistence on a 6:30 a.m. start time. I watched them. I listened hard. A lot of what we talked about focused on surrender: giving up the old baggage, the distractions, the beliefs that no longer served them. The goal was to get closer to living our own uniquely divine lives. No one in the group, no matter how successful he'd been, was unscathed or unscarred. Everyone came with a limp."

LIVING OUR LIVES TOGETHER

Today, those "cockpit conversations" continue in my living room on FaceTime or Zoom. We select a thought or passage from one of our daily reading books that sparks meaningful comments. We explore our personal beliefs, expose our deep feelings and reflect on the bigger picture. When we are sharing at this level, we are on the vertical path that Eckhart Tolle talks about: we discover awakening and awareness and we are close to the God of our understanding. Gems of discovery surface. We are intimate. We trust each other and what is shared in the circle stays in the circle. No exceptions.

Ultimately, we seek to explore feelings rather than just details of the "plot" of our life stories. This approach is definitely counter-culture, but it is profoundly humanizing. It lets each participant be seen and heard—not simply acknowledged as a character in a story, but as a feeling person who is navigating the bewildering and beautiful process of growing older with others who are willing to share the journey.

By contrast, when Yvonne and I attend cocktail parties, if I meet people who aren't willing to talk about the substance of their lives, I politely tune out. I'm an introvert and not very social anyway. I want to have intimate relationships, not engage in small talk.

When we reach the final years of our lives, our job is to be more present and to live in the here and now. We're not *Doing*; we are *Being*. This is how I believe we can make our best contributions as we age.

DOING DIFFERENTLY

I have found that giving up control has led me to a new sense of freedom that has released me to explore this new territory called "retirement" and owning my status as an elder. At the same time, I am sometimes forced to be idle and I know that I'm not needed the way I used to be. I play with our grandchildren, take stock of my life, and practice mindfulness. There are few societal rewards for what I am *Being*, rather than *Doing* in my new-found time.

Aging has also prompted me to think about my legacy, not just in terms of material possessions and financial independence, but in terms of values and memories. What do I want my children and grandchildren to remember? For me, it's not about wealth or accomplishments; it's about love, resilience and gratitude. Part of my legacy is this book—a reflection on my journey through life's seasons. It is my hope that my words will inspire my family to live with courage and grace.

All my life, I focused on project dreams, talking about them and making them successful. Fortunately, with aging, I no longer care so much about what other people think about me or what I'm doing…and that's freeing! I can dare to be as open and honest as I've ever been.

I am also conscious of fear as I age and I'm willing to talk openly about going blind or facing death with my closest friends.

With decades in recovery, I continue to practice surrender, although my focus is no longer solely on my active addiction. Now I am surrendering to the inevitable changes that I face as I age. As I do this, I work at letting go of my ego and false self with its grasping, unrealistic expectations, so that I can remain my true self. My ego will not save me from the predictable losses of aging and death, but my recovery program—and my peers who walk the same path—will help me face my end.

Ram Dass, born Richard Alpert, who worked in spiritual growth and taught workshops on conscious aging and dying (Elisabeth Kubler-Ross was a student) said this about aging and death: "We are all just walking each other home."

I can move outside my body and observe aging and share the details of what I see with my close friends who are also using their 12-Step and other spiritual programs to stay grounded as the years pass. We are genuinely Real with each other.

"You become. It takes a long time.
That's why it doesn't happen often to people
Who break easily, or have sharp edges,
Or who have to be carefully kept.
Generally, by the time you are Real,
Most of your hair has been loved off,
And your eyes drop out,
And you get loose in your joints…
And very shabby.
But these things don't matter at all,
Because once you are Real, you can't be ugly,
Except to people who don't understand."

Margery Williams *The Velveteen Rabbit* 1922

GETTING REAL: STRUGGLES AND SUFFERING

I will continue to experience a wrestling match with fear and resistance until I can accept life as it is, surrender completely and let go.

I will never do this perfectly.

Steps One, Two and Three of my 12-Step program tell me this (adapted here from Alcoholics Anonymous using my language):

- I am powerless over the rigors of aging, but my life doesn't have to be unmanageable, because…
- A power greater than I will restore me to sanity, especially when I'm scared and struggling,
- If I turn my will and my life over to the care of God as I understand God, one day at a time (…and sometimes minutes at a time, if need be) grace happens: I am given a gift from the God of my understanding that I did not earn.

For me, meditation and quiet prayer focused on these three concepts is my answer to remaining on the "vertical plane" more and more. When I do this, I can receive the gift of acceptance even when I struggle and suffer.

RESISTANCE SPAWNS SUFFERING

After decades in recovery, I still face struggles: moments when fear and anxiety creep in, despite my best efforts.

In 2022, for example, Hurricane Ian struck, a category 5 storm with 160 mph winds causing damage totaling $112 billion as the storm moved through the Caribbean, into Florida just south of us, and then into the Carolinas, killing 161 people. About the same time, the U.S. financial markets took a sharp downturn. These two events reminded me how easily fear can take hold if I let it and I have learned a key lesson. Suffering is often tied to a "guest," as poet/philosopher Rumi calls it: "The dark thought, the shame, the malice…" but I can "meet them at the door…Be grateful for whatever comes," Rumi reminds us, "because each has been sent as a guide from beyond."

Only two years later, it happened again. Hurricane winds and flood waters can inflict catastrophic damage in coastal areas and Hurricane Milton, arriving in October 2024, packed that punch. Though our town, Venice, didn't receive a direct hit, the storm still carried Category 3 winds of 111 to 129 mph at landfall. With a stern warning of substantial storm surge and torrential rains, we made the decision to evacuate our home and travel to Orlando. While our neighborhood was spared, the wind gusts—as high as

150 mph—flattened trees, destroyed roofs and downed power lines.

Remarkably, our beach home endured no structural damage but the storm surge left two feet of standing water on our lawn. Fortunately, our outdoor swimming pool, elevated by three feet, acted as a crucial water barrier so it wasn't inundated with the potentially destructive salt water. Our grass and landscaping, however, was not spared: the salt intrusion "burned" the grass and ornamental plantings. We replaced most of our front yard.

We were lucky. An abnormal rise of water pushed onto shore by strong winds called a storm surge can be deadly and overcome an entire neighborhood in mere hours. That didn't happen. All around us, however, our Venice community showed signs of the weather assault: damaged piers, debris-strewn streets and sand-choked beaches. Our home remained intact, our belongings were unharmed and, most importantly, we were safe. Only one mile away from us, however, in the neighborhood where we once lived, homes were totally destroyed by ocean water that rose several feet.

Natural disasters like these have taught me to find strength in surrendering control. Here is the real truth: we all have far less control than we think. When I can accept reality in its totality and trust in God's plan, peace actually becomes possible, even in the worst of times, and that includes hurricanes.

LETTING GO IS A SACRED ACT

I am definitely feeling the passage of time: not in a negative way, but in my choices to slow down and reflect. I recognize that "the old man" is knocking and—instead of ignoring him—I've decided to open the door, laugh and invite him in. I might as well enjoy his company. It is strange and fascinating that I can, at times, almost separate myself from my body.

Aging means giving up control, practicing acceptance and saying goodbye to things we once loved.

These transitions have not been easy or entirely welcome for me. Few people would choose the challenges that come with aging over the vitality of midlife, yet it is still better than the alternative: not being here at all. The struggles we face with aging are directly tied to our resistance to reality, but when we let go of resistance and embrace acceptance, we open ourselves up to deeper love—for ourselves and for others. At the same time, aging invites us to make space for new joys, deeper gratitude and the quiet wisdom that change can bring.

Aging offers us a chance to awaken spiritually by confronting our fears: fear of irrelevance, fear of fragility and decline, fear of death itself. This process isn't easy: it requires courage and self-reflection. By letting go of attachments, both material and emotional, we free ourselves from unnecessary suffering. This freedom allows us to love more deeply with greater generosity toward family, friends…and even ourselves.

Recently, I gave up driving due to my worsening vision from glaucoma. Three years ago at 84, I said farewell to some of my greatest passions—those heart-pounding hikes and exhilarating mountain road bike rides through the wild beauty of Vail, Colorado. Two years ago, I hung up my biking gear and retired my snow skis. Not long after that we sold *Serenity 2*, our beloved sailing yacht. That marked the end of 40 years of exploring the Caribbean: a time filled with salt air, stars and rare freedom that only the sea can offer.

Each of these transitions were difficult, but in every case they invited me to practice the sacred art of release. I'm learning that letting go of what I love isn't just a physical act: it is deeply emotional and it mirrors our very existence. My abilities have slowed down in all areas and I recognize this. I'm grateful that I can step outside my body, look at myself and say kindly, "Hey Burt, you're slowin' down. You can't walk as far or run as fast. Take a nap on the couch. That's what happens with age."

LET OTHERS TAKE THE LEAD

I feel less relevant and that word carries its own quiet grief, especially for a guy who always made things happen. Others take the lead now with decisions I once instinctively handled. It is humbling to surrender these familiar roles. I am reminded, however, that we who live in the final chapters of our lives, also have immense life experience and knowledge to share, when we are asked.

Aging can diminish the size of our world with physical limits and fewer plans, but I believe that the rewards of living never cease. As a former athlete, I'm in tune with my body and I have a high level of awareness that my recovery program gives me. I have learned to live one day at a time. My mind is still sound. I have no feelings of regret or sadness. I'm grateful for the health I have at 87.

My ego will not save me from the predictable suffering of aging and death. I will live my life with my true self, not my false self. I am watching the world move a little faster without waiting for me to catch up. Life is constantly evolving and—if I hold too tight—I cannot live fully in the present. By releasing my attachments, whether physical or emotional, I can find greater freedom and serenity. Life is rewarding, even if I'm slowing down.

CHOOSE GRATITUDE

It is important to focus on gratitude for what we have, rather than mourn the endings. In the summer of 2025, when Yvonne visited Vail with our family, the 8,000-foot, thin mountain air was especially challenging for me. Here was the air that once restored me and now it left me gasping. We could not deny the truth. Facing this loss of a favorite "home place" might have felt like a defeat, but we both embraced the treasure of more time at sea level instead.

Rather than mourning what we left behind, I celebrate what I am so lucky to have: energizing swims in a pool a few steps from the Atlantic gulf coast, two-mile walks into our little town, my 15-minute morning Pilates routine and a little weight lifting for good measure. These daily rituals fill my days with vitality and joy. I'm still here, I remind myself with a smile…and I'm still me.

Yvonne and I have been happily married for 35 harmonious years. Two keys to our happiness are acceptance and learning to let go of control. Now we spend most of our time in Venice, Florida. When we visit Vail, Yvonne continues to ski each year and I cherish my time at a lower altitude with our long-time friends and family who live there. Acceptance has made all the difference. Instead of Vail as our summer and holiday destination, we now visit Minnesota where many of our family members live.

ONE DAY AT A TIME

Decades of recovery in my 12-Step program have anchored me in a simple, powerful truth: live one day at a time. This practice carries me through every change, every moment of suffering and surrender, every rebirth. I awake each morning with deeper gratitude—for my steady breath, for the light I can see, for the privilege of aging with awareness and dignity.

At 87, I am living life at a slower, gentler rhythm and it is a change that I welcome. My years in recovery have taught me acceptance, gratitude and resilience and these qualities have guided me though this stage of aging with steadiness and clarity.

Age has also taught me that we will step out of the spotlight with aging and I have discovered freedom in that shift. I have fewer demands, I am unhurried and I have more room simply to *be*. My glaucoma means I often need an arm, but the support of Yvonne, my 5 children and 12 grandchildren makes these moments feel less like limitations and more like reminders of our closeness.

My fears of blindness and even of death have softened. I have been given the great gift of love, purpose and connection in my 87 years.

LIVING HAPPY, JOYOUS AND FREE

WONDERS IN MULTIPLES

With 26 family members, my recovery life has brought me closer to what truly matters: family. Not only has recovery extended my life, it has made me a far better husband, father and grandfather. I am a person that my family wants to be around.

As we age, our lives can become narrower and self-absorbed without even noticing it. Here is another benefit of my recovery program. I am required to listen to others, to hear their truths and keep those "helpful" suggestions to myself (unless asked).

With my 12 grandchildren, I take the initiative. I really want to know what is going on in their lives. We share interests: even though we live in different states. My grandsons and I love to watch the Vikings games together and share play-by-play remarks via texts. When I see the videos, I'm amazed by our granddaughter Samara's growing expertise as she refines her skills in dance and theater and prepares for a performing arts major in college. I've also become a volleyball fan because our granddaughter Murphy not only plays on her high school team in St. Paul, but she has been invited to participate in an advanced league that draws athletes from around the U.S.

Every one of our grandchildren knows that when something really matters in their lives, they will have my undivided attention.

Our large, extended family gathers in Florida every June, after school is out and, for more than 30 years, we have shared one, major New Year trip. This cherished tradition first took us to Vail, next to Mexico for several years, and, in 2026, we will all land in Costa Rica. Typically, we rent a large house to accommodate everyone, always located beside a beach with a big swimming pool.

Yvonne and I have also taken at least one, yearly international trip together for the past three decades. Most recently, we visited Botswana and Mozambique in Southern Africa in 2024 and boarded the Golden Eagle Express luxury train traveling to Budapest, Hungary and Vienna, Austria, with stops in Poland, Germany and the Czech Republic in August 2025.

This pace at 87 is not without its challenges. Truth be told, traveling at any age can test one's patience with long international flights, crowded airports, heavy luggage and the ever-present jet lag. Experience has taught Yvonne and I to manage tense moments when our feelings threaten to collide. I learned this four-word prayer many years ago and I use it liberally: "Bless her, Change me."

Over the years, I've trained myself to rest on planes, which lessens the effect of time changes. Small habits like this make all the difference and they prepare us to arrive energized and ready to explore.

Yvonne and I intend to continue traveling internationally for as long as we are physically able. Far from being tiring, these journeys seem to invigorate me. Travel ignites my energy, sharpens my mind, and motivates me to keep up with even the most demanding sightseeing schedules. Each trip reminds me that age does not have to close the door on adventure—it can, instead, open the door to a deeper appreciation of the world.

SIMPLY GRATEFUL

As I age in recovery, I am abundantly grateful for what truly matters: our growing family of adult children, their partners and grandchildren. Every one of them has been raised with considerable privilege and guaranteed financial security, yet each of them is responsible, willing to work hard and give back to their communities.

The most exciting part is that Yvonne and I love them all… and they love us back.

Jennie and Jane, now retired, have five boys, Nick, Sam, Ikey, Michael and Gabe who are thriving in their own individual pursuits and making their parents proud. Nick and Becky were married in Los Angeles in 2021.

Jennie and Jane's family home is in St. Paul, Minnesota, with a beautiful log cabin retreat in northern Wisconsin where we have enjoyed countless family gatherings in the woods near Minong, a village south of Lake Superior.

John and Tammy live in Vail, Colorado, where John still works as a ski technician. John is gearing up for retirement so that he can design and build their new summer cabin near Hayward, Wisconsin. Their children, Seth and Sonny, are completing their final years of college and Samara studies dance and theater at the Vail Mountain School.

Katie and Rob are busy bringing their beautiful home in St. Paul up-to-date. Rob continues working in the medical field and their children, Murphy and Jack, attend Saint Paul Academy, and pursue their fierce interests in volleyball and basketball.

Anne Marie and Aaron live in Marin County, California and were married on August 8, 2025 in the Palace of Fine Arts in downtown San Francisco. They have been building a strong, blended family with Anne's two boys—Les and Joel—and Aaron's two girls—Gillian (Gilly) and Sofia. The love among them is unmistakable.

Brian, hockey coach at the University of St. Thomas, and Jordan, working in the medical field, flew to Hawaii in July, 2025 to marry—just the two of them. In August we celebrated with a wedding reception of more than 150 people in Katie's St. Paul backyard, a beautiful, successful event.

In October, 2025, Yvonne and I flew to Knoxville, Tennessee, to meet Jennie, Jane and our grandson, Sam, and his fiancee, Chloe. We visited the venue for their upcoming wedding in 2026: the Smoky Mountains, part of the ancient Appalachian Mountain Range.

Yvonne and I have so much to look forward to as we witness the engaged and contributing lives of our adult children, their partners and the amazing unfolding lives of our 12 grandchildren. We are blessed beyond measure and thankful every day.

WITNESS TO THE GREATEST GENERATION

As I look back on my life, I cannot help but marvel at the world that we live in today. I have been fortunate to live not in one, but two centuries. In writing this book, I wanted to share not only my story, but also underscore my deep appreciation for the extraordinary times I have witnessed and experienced. Imagine advancements like these:

- From party-line telephones to video calls,
- From vinyl records to streaming music,
- From handwritten letters to instant messages.

I believe that the past eight decades have been the greatest era in world history to be alive so far. These decades have brought us longer lives, unimagined technology, greater prosperity and a more inclusive society.

My grandparents spoke of a time when people rarely lived past their 50s and now I am 87, still active and grateful for every day. Over the past 100 years, Americans could only expect to live about 55 years. Today, the realistic expectation is nearly 80. Advances in medicine, better nutrition and improved public health have made all the difference.

I have seen first-hand treatment for diseases that once seemed insurmountable and they are routine today. I have watched friends and family live longer, healthier lives and I am thankful for the care and scientific knowledge that has made this possible.

During my lifetime, we have also seen unprecedented technological innovation, changing every aspect of our daily lives. Much of this progress was ignited during and after World War II as technologies were adapted for civilian life, leading to breakthroughs in computing, materials science and telecommunications.

The rise of personal computers, the internet and smart phones have revolutionized communications, work and access to information. Today, technologies such as artificial intelligence and cloud computing are reshaping industries and improving our quality of life.

When I was young, many families struggled to make ends meet. Now, most of us enjoy comforts and opportunities that would have been unimaginable to my parents. In the U.S., the standard of living has improved dramatically. I've seen homes become more comfortable, food become more safe, nutritious and plentiful and opportunities for education and travel expand dramatically. The economy has grown and, with it, our ability to care for ourselves and for each other. I am grateful for the security and abundance that has marked my life.

Society has changed in remarkable ways. When I was growing up, many doors were closed to people because of who they were, where they came from, their sex or the color of their skin. Today, we are more aware of the importance of equity and inclusion. Social programs have expanded and education is more accessible. We are working toward a more just and safer world for all.

As I share my story of grace and aging in recovery, I hope to inspire my children, grandchildren and others to appreciate the gifts of our time and face the future with hope and graditude.

DEATH AND DYING: A GRACEFUL REFLECTION

My true self—not my false self or ego—will carry me through the end of my own fleeting appearance in this life. My thoughts about what comes next have been influenced by my recovery journey: the spiritual awakening that made me believe in a Higher Power and my belief that my journey will continue after this one. My body today is simply a carrier of my soul and my spirit.

I wasn't raised in a family that believed in an afterlife. In fact, the god of my childhood was a fire and brimstone, damning god. I grew up to be a non-believer with no thought given to faith until I started my recovery journey from addiction. Now, I am open to the mystery of death. I believe it is possible to prepare ourselves consciously for our own passing and to spend our last days with love in our hearts and the kind of support surrounding us that will help us make the transition.

Some people believe that we simply end when this life, as we know it, ends; after all the complexity, mystery and wonder of being human, nothing follows. As I look back on my 87 years as a human being, the idea that such a sophisticated creation—call it a machine, if you will—could just wink out after 70 or 80 years rings hollow for me.

My conviction about what comes next is this:

I have lived an amazing, unlikely and truly beautiful life. I have known laughter, heartbreak, loss, achievement and miraculous love. I genuinely believe there is more waiting for us after our old, tired bodies wear out.

My first 40 years were a wild expedition: exploring, accumulating, pushing boundaries, sometimes seeking escape through chemicals that changed how I felt. I was always searching, always hungry for more. But at 40, everything changed. I found the 12-Step program and it transformed every aspect of my existence. It wasn't that the first part of my life was bad or regrettable; far from it. But the second act became gentler, simpler, softer—marked by living one day at a time and leaning into a Higher Power for guidance.

I believe none of this was accidental.

We are all born happy and our souls are unburdened, but we often live complicated lives tangled in fear, the urge to control, character blemishes and the full palette of human flaws.

I hold on to the belief that when our bodies have lived long enough, we will return to a state of peace. This is what aging with grace means to me: facing death not with fear, but with thankfulness for the journey, trust in the next chapter, and a heart full of love that refuses to die.

I will meet those who traveled ahead of me and I promise to send some small sign, some signal, to those I love: a reminder that love transcends even death and nothing beautiful is ever, truly gone. These promises have come true in my life since I found recovery. I am grateful beyond measure.

THE PROMISES

If we are painstaking about this phase of our development, we will be amazed before we are half way through.

We are going to know a new freedom and a new happiness.

We will not regret the past nor wish to shut the door on it.

We will comprehend the word serenity and we will know peace.

No matter how far down the scale we have gone, we will see how our experience can benefit others.

That feeling of uselessness and self-pity will disappear.

We will lose interest in selfish things and gain interest in our fellows.

Self-seeking will slip away.

Our whole attitude and outlook upon life with change.

Fear of people and of economic insecurity will leave us.

We will intuitively know how to handle situations which used to baffle us.

We will suddenly realize that God is doing for us what we could not do for ourselves.

Are these extravagant promises? We think not. They are being fulfilled among us—sometimes quickly, sometimes slowly. They will always materialize if we work for them.

From the *Big Book of Alcoholics Anonymous* pages 83-84

I will close with this promise from the mystic and poet Rumi:

"Out beyond ideas of wrongdoing and rightdoing,
there is a field.
I will meet you there."

THE TWELVE STEPS OF ALCOHOLICS ANONYMOUS

1. We admitted we were powerless over alcohol—that our lives had become unmanageable.
2. Came to believe that a Power greater than ourselves could restore us to sanity.
3. Made a decision to turn our will and our lives over to the care of God as we understood Him.
4. Made a searching and fearless moral inventory of ourselves.
5. Admitted to God, to ourselves, and to another human being the exact nature of our wrongs.
6. Were entirely ready to have God remove all these defects of character.
7. Humbly asked Him to remove our shortcomings.
8. Made a list of all persons we had harmed, and became willing to make amends to them all.
9. Made direct amends to such people wherever possible, except when to do so would injure them or others.
10. Continued to take personal inventory and when we were wrong promptly admitted it.
11. Sought through prayer and meditation to improve our conscious contact with God as we understood Him, praying only for knowledge of His will for us and the power to carry that out.
12. Having had a spiritual awakening as a result of these Steps, we tried to carry this message to alcoholics, and to practice these principles in all our affairs.

THE TWELVE STEPS OF OVEREATERS ANONYMOUS

1. We admitted we were powerless over food—that our lives had become unmanageable.
2. Came to believe that a Power greater than ourselves could restore us to sanity.
3. Made a decision to turn our will and our lives over to the care of God as we understood Him.
4. Made a searching and fearless moral inventory of ourselves.
5. Admitted to God, to ourselves, and to another human being the exact nature of our wrongs.
6. Were entirely ready to have God remove all these defects of character.
7. Humbly asked Him to remove our shortcomings.
8. Made a list of all persons we had harmed, and became willing to make amends to them all.
9. Made direct amends to such people wherever possible, except when to do so would injure them or others.
10. Continued to take personal inventory and when we were wrong promptly admitted it.
11. Sought through prayer and meditation to improve our conscious contact with God as we understood Him, praying only for knowledge of His will for us and the power to carry that out.
12. Having had a spiritual awakening as a result of these Steps, we tried to carry this message to compulsive overeaters, and to practice these principles in all our affairs.